A Blueprint for Launching Your Own Business

From Concept to Success – Practical Strategies, Tips, and Tools for Aspiring Entrepreneurs

Jasper Wrenwood

Table of content

Chapter one
Introduction

Embarking on the journey of starting a new business is a thrilling endeavor that demands passion, dedication, and a strategic approach. Welcome to "Venture Ignition: A Blueprint for Launching Your Own Business," where we will guide you through the intricacies of turning your entrepreneurial dreams into a reality. In this comprehensive guide, we will explore the key steps, strategies, and essential elements required to build a successful business from the ground up.

The entrepreneurial journey is a road less traveled, filled with both excitement and challenges. As you stand at the threshold of this adventure, it's crucial to recognize the significance of laying a solid foundation for your business. This introduction serves as a compass, pointing you towards the critical aspects of business development and providing insights that will prove invaluable on your path to success.

In the initial chapters, we will delve into the process of defining your business concept. Identifying your passion and expertise is the starting point, allowing you to align your venture with what truly inspires and motivates you. We'll also explore the importance of market research, helping you discover a niche and analyze demand –

essential elements that contribute to a business's long-term viability.

A cornerstone of any successful business is a well-crafted business plan. Section three will guide you through the elements that constitute a robust plan, from outlining your mission and vision to developing financial projections and funding strategies. Understanding the intricacies of your business on paper is the key to attracting investors, partners, and customers.

Legal and regulatory considerations can be daunting, but in section four, we break down the complexities. Choosing the right business structure, navigating licensing requirements, and ensuring compliance with regulations are crucial steps that will set the stage for a legally sound and sustainable business.

Building a recognizable and trustworthy brand is explored in section five. Crafting a unique value proposition and implementing effective branding strategies are essential for standing out in a competitive market. Your brand is not just a logo; it's the promise and experience you deliver to your customers.

Setting up and managing operations is the focus of section six. From choosing the right location to establishing efficient supply chain management, these operational decisions lay the groundwork for a smooth and effective business process. Additionally, we delve into the importance of inventory management to avoid common pitfalls.

In the subsequent sections, we explore marketing and sales strategies, financial management, and the intricacies of hiring and managing teams. These aspects are crucial components of your business's day-to-day operations, contributing to its overall success and growth.

As you progress through the guide, we address the challenges that often accompany the entrepreneurial journey. Section eleven emphasizes the importance of resilience, learning from failures, and adapting to change. By understanding common pitfalls and embracing a growth mindset, you'll be better equipped to overcome obstacles and navigate the evolving landscape of entrepreneurship.

In conclusion, "Venture Ignition" is more than a guide; it's a roadmap to transforming your business aspirations into a thriving reality. Celebrate the milestones, learn from the challenges, and embrace the continuous evolution of your business. The journey ahead is both exhilarating and transformative, and we are here to accompany you every step of the way.

1.1 Welcome to the Entrepreneurial Journey

Embarking on the entrepreneurial journey is akin to setting sail on uncharted waters, where every decision becomes a navigation point, and each challenge an opportunity for growth. Welcome to a transformative experience, where your ideas, passion, and determination converge to shape a business of your own.

In this dynamic landscape, the entrepreneurial journey is not merely a destination; it's a continuous exploration of possibilities, a journey where innovation meets determination. As you step into this realm, envision the path ahead as a canvas waiting for your unique strokes. Your entrepreneurial spirit is the compass that will guide you through the twists and turns of this exhilarating expedition.

The entrepreneurial journey is marked by a sense of purpose, a driving force that compels you to turn dreams into reality. It's about identifying gaps in the market, recognizing opportunities, and daring to create something meaningful. Each step forward is a testament to your vision, resilience, and commitment to making a difference.

In the vast landscape of entrepreneurship, diversity reigns supreme. Whether you're a seasoned professional venturing into a new endeavor or a budding entrepreneur filled with enthusiasm, the journey is uniquely yours. It's an odyssey that welcomes innovators, risk-takers, and those who believe in the transformative power of their ideas.

As you take your first steps, remember that challenges are an integral part of the entrepreneurial journey. These challenges are not roadblocks but rather stepping stones that propel you forward. They test your mettle, refine your strategies, and ultimately contribute to the resilience that defines successful entrepreneurs.

The entrepreneurial journey is a learning curve, an educational expedition where every experience, success, and setback becomes a lesson. It's an environment that encourages adaptability, curiosity, and a willingness to embrace change. The ability to pivot and evolve is not just an option; it's a necessity in a landscape that is as dynamic as it is rewarding.

Networking and collaboration are foundational to the entrepreneurial journey. Surrounding yourself with a supportive community, mentors, and like-minded individuals amplifies your capacity to innovate and overcome obstacles. The exchange of ideas, insights, and shared experiences creates a synergy that propels you forward, even in the face of uncertainty.

Welcome to a journey that celebrates the entrepreneurial spirit – a spirit that challenges the status quo, pushes boundaries, and envisions a future where your ideas contribute to the greater tapestry of innovation. As you embark on this expedition, know that you are not alone. Countless entrepreneurs have traversed similar paths, leaving behind a trail of inspiration, lessons, and success stories.

In "Venture Ignition: A Blueprint for Launching Your Own Business," we are here to accompany you on this transformative odyssey. Each chapter unfolds new insights, strategies, and tools to empower you on your entrepreneurial journey. Let this guide be your companion, offering guidance and support as you navigate the exciting and challenging terrain of building your own business. The journey begins now, and the possibilities are limitless.

1.2 The Importance of a Solid Business Foundation

A solid business foundation is the bedrock upon which successful enterprises are built, providing stability, structure, and a roadmap for sustained growth. Understanding and prioritizing the elements that contribute to this foundation is paramount for any entrepreneur venturing into the dynamic world of business.

First and foremost, a well-defined business concept forms the cornerstone of a solid foundation. Clarity regarding your products or services, target audience, and the value you offer is essential. This clarity not only guides your initial steps but also becomes the anchor that aligns all aspects of your business strategy.

Market research is the scaffolding that supports a business's foundation. Thoroughly understanding the market landscape, identifying competitors, and gauging consumer needs and trends are integral components. This knowledge empowers entrepreneurs to position their businesses strategically, uncover unmet demands, and make informed decisions that resonate with their target audience.

Crafting a comprehensive business plan is akin to drawing up the blueprints for a sturdy structure. This plan outlines your mission, vision, and objectives, providing a roadmap for achieving goals. It encompasses financial projections, operational strategies, and a clear path for scalability. Investors, partners, and even your own team will look to this plan as a guiding document, emphasizing the importance of its meticulous development.

Legal and regulatory considerations constitute the protective walls around your business foundation. Selecting the right business structure, whether it be a sole proprietorship, partnership, LLC, or corporation, has profound implications for liability, taxation, and overall organizational efficiency. Complying with licensing requirements and regulations ensures a solid legal footing, shielding your business from potential pitfalls.

A recognizable and trustworthy brand acts as the facade of your business foundation. Building a brand goes beyond creating a logo; it involves defining your unique value proposition, establishing a brand personality, and cultivating a positive brand image. A strong brand resonates with your target audience, fostering loyalty and setting the stage for long-term success.

Setting up and managing operations is the infrastructure that supports day-to-day activities. From selecting an appropriate location to implementing efficient supply chain management, operational decisions influence your business's efficiency and customer satisfaction. Proper inventory management ensures a smooth flow of products or services, preventing disruptions that can undermine your foundation.

In essence, the importance of a solid business foundation lies in its ability to withstand the tests of time and external challenges. It provides entrepreneurs with a sense of direction, stability, and a framework for decision-making. Just as a well-constructed building relies on a strong foundation to weather storms, a business with a solid foundation is better equipped to navigate the uncertainties of the market and industry changes.

As we embark on the journey of "Venture Ignition," it is crucial to recognize that each subsequent chapter builds upon the principles of a solid business foundation. From legal considerations to brand development and operational strategies, this guide is designed to fortify your understanding and implementation of these foundational elements, setting the stage for a resilient and thriving business.

Chapter Two
Defining Your Business Concept

Defining your business concept is the pivotal first step in transforming your entrepreneurial vision into a tangible and viable venture. This process involves a deliberate exploration of your passion, expertise, and the market landscape to craft a clear and compelling identity for your business.

At the heart of defining your business concept is a deep introspection into your passions and skills. What drives you? What are you genuinely enthusiastic about? Identifying these core elements ensures that your business is not only a financial endeavor but also a reflection of your personal values and interests. This alignment sets the foundation for a sustainable and fulfilling entrepreneurial journey.

Market research is the compass that guides your business concept toward a receptive audience. Understanding your target market, analyzing consumer needs, and identifying potential gaps in the market landscape are crucial steps. By conducting thorough research, you position your business to address real-world demands, increasing its relevance and potential for success.

The unique value proposition (UVP) is the beacon that distinguishes your business concept in a crowded marketplace. What sets your products or services apart? Why should customers choose your business over competitors? Articulating a compelling UVP not only attracts customers but also forms the basis for your branding and marketing strategies.

A clearly defined target audience is another critical facet of your business concept. Tailoring your products or services to meet the specific needs and preferences of a well-defined audience enhances your chances of resonating with potential customers. Knowing your audience intimately allows you to craft marketing messages that speak directly to their interests and concerns.

As you define your business concept, it's essential to assess its feasibility. This involves evaluating the resources required, potential challenges, and the scalability of your idea. A realistic understanding of the practical aspects of your concept ensures that you can navigate the complexities of bringing it to life effectively.

In "Venture Ignition," the chapter on defining your business concept serves as a guide through these crucial steps. From identifying your passion to conducting

market research and shaping a compelling UVP, each
component contributes to the clarity and strength of your
business concept. This chapter aims to empower you
with the knowledge and tools needed to articulate a
concept that not only aligns with your vision but also
resonates with your target audience, laying the
groundwork for a successful entrepreneurial journey.

2.1 Identifying Your Passion and Expertise

Identifying your passion and expertise is the cornerstone
of building a business that aligns with your personal
fulfillment and professional strengths. This introspective
journey involves recognizing what truly motivates and
inspires you, paving the way for a business venture that
goes beyond mere financial gain.

Passion is the driving force that propels entrepreneurs to
overcome challenges and persevere in the face of
adversity. Take a moment to reflect on what excites you,
what activities bring you joy, and where your genuine
interests lie. Whether it's a hobby, a cause, or a specific
industry, your passion should serve as the compass
guiding your entrepreneurial endeavors.

Expertise complements passion by leveraging your
skills, knowledge, and experience. Identify areas where

you excel, whether through formal education, work experience, or personal development. Your expertise is a valuable asset that not only sets you apart from others but also instills confidence in your ability to navigate the intricacies of your chosen field.

The intersection of passion and expertise is the sweet spot where your business concept gains authenticity and depth. When you build a business around what you love and what you excel at, your commitment becomes more than a strategic decision – it becomes a genuine reflection of who you are. This alignment not only fuels your dedication but also resonates with customers who appreciate authenticity and passion in the businesses they support.

As you embark on the journey of identifying your passion and expertise in "Venture Ignition," consider this chapter as a guide to self-discovery. Through exercises and insights, you'll uncover the elements that drive you and the areas where you naturally excel. This foundational step sets the stage for a business venture that is not only financially rewarding but also personally fulfilling, ensuring that your entrepreneurial journey is a holistic and gratifying experience.

2.2 Market Research: Finding a Niche and Analyzing Demand

Market research is the compass that guides your entrepreneurial journey, providing essential insights into the landscape where your business will thrive. Finding a niche and analyzing demand are critical components of this process, helping you identify opportunities, understand customer needs, and position your venture strategically.

Finding a niche involves pinpointing a specific segment of the market where your products or services can stand out. This could be an underserved audience, an unexplored product category, or a unique approach to an existing market. By carving out a niche, your business gains a competitive edge and becomes more appealing to a targeted audience.

Analyzing demand goes hand in hand with finding a niche. Understanding what customers want, their preferences, and the problems they seek to solve allows you to tailor your offerings effectively. Through surveys, interviews, and data analysis, you can gather valuable information about market trends, customer behaviors, and potential gaps that your business can fill.

Market research is not a one-time activity but an ongoing process. Regularly monitoring market trends and customer feedback ensures that your business remains adaptive and responsive to changes. By staying attuned to shifts in demand, emerging technologies, and evolving consumer preferences, you position your venture for long-term success.

In "Venture Ignition," the chapter on market research serves as a comprehensive guide to navigating these crucial steps. From defining your target market and assessing competition to conducting surveys and analyzing data, this chapter equips you with the tools to make informed decisions. By the end, you'll have a clear understanding of your business's niche and a nuanced view of the demand you aim to meet, setting the stage for a purposeful and market-savvy entrepreneurial venture.

Chapter Three
Crafting a Comprehensive Business Plan

Crafting a comprehensive business plan is a pivotal step on the entrepreneurial journey, providing a structured roadmap for your venture's success. This detailed document serves as a guide, outlining your business's mission, vision, strategies, and financial projections. It is not only a tool for internal decision-making but also a crucial document for attracting investors, partners, and other stakeholders.

The elements of a comprehensive business plan include:

1. **Executive Summary:**
- A concise overview of your business, highlighting its key components and objectives.

2. **Business Description:**
- A detailed explanation of your business concept, its mission, and the problems it aims to solve.

3. **Market Analysis:**
- In-depth research on your target market, industry trends, and an analysis of competitors.

4. **Organization and Management:**
- Insights into your business's structure, leadership team, and key personnel.

5. **Products or Services:**
- A comprehensive description of what your business offers, highlighting unique features and benefits.

6. **Marketing and Sales Strategies:**
- Plans for promoting and selling your products or services, including target demographics and marketing channels.

7. **Funding Request (if applicable):**
- Details about your financial needs, including funding requirements and use of funds.

8. **Financial Projections:**
- Forecasts for revenue, expenses, and profits over a specific period, typically three to five years.

9. **Appendix:**
- Supplementary materials such as resumes, additional financial data, or market research details.

Crafting each section meticulously not only helps you clarify your business's direction but also serves as a valuable communication tool when seeking external support. Investors and lenders often scrutinize business plans to assess the viability and potential of the venture.

In "Venture Ignition," the chapter on crafting a comprehensive business plan guides you through each aspect of this critical document. From defining your business model to projecting financials and outlining marketing strategies, this chapter aims to empower you with the tools needed to create a robust business plan. As you progress through this stage, keep in mind that your business plan is a living document, subject to updates and revisions as your venture evolves and grows.

3.1 Elements of a Strong Business Plan

A strong business plan is a well-structured document that communicates the viability, strategies, and potential of your business. Here are key elements that contribute to the strength of a comprehensive business plan:

1. **Executive Summary:**
- Concise overview of your business, summarizing its mission, goals, and key components.

2. **Business Description:**
- Detailed explanation of your business concept, mission statement, and the problems it aims to address.

3. **Market Analysis:**
- In-depth research on your target market, industry trends, and analysis of competitors.

4. **Organization and Management:**

- Insight into your business's structure, leadership team, key personnel, and their roles.

5. **Products or Services:**
- Comprehensive description of what your business offers, emphasizing unique features and benefits.

6. **Marketing and Sales Strategies:**
- Plans for promoting and selling your products or services, including target demographics and marketing channels.

7. **Funding Request (if applicable):**
- Details about your financial needs, including funding requirements and how the funds will be used.

8. **Financial Projections:**
- Forecasts for revenue, expenses, and profits over a specific period, typically three to five years.

9. **Appendix:**
- Supplementary materials, such as resumes, additional financial data, or detailed market research.

Each element serves a specific purpose in providing a comprehensive understanding of your business to potential stakeholders. The executive summary is often the first impression, capturing the essence of your business. The market analysis and competition assessment demonstrate your awareness of the industry landscape. The organizational structure highlights the key players and their roles, instilling confidence in your management team.

The description of your products or services delves into what sets your offerings apart, while marketing and sales strategies showcase your plans for reaching and attracting customers. If seeking funding, the funding request section outlines the financial support you're looking for, and financial projections provide a glimpse into the anticipated financial performance of your business.

The appendix serves as a repository for supplementary materials that support and enhance the information presented in the main sections.

In "Venture Ignition," the chapter on crafting a comprehensive business plan provides detailed insights into developing each of these elements. By meticulously addressing these components, you create a robust business plan that not only guides your internal operations but also becomes a valuable tool when presenting your business to external stakeholders.

3.2 Financial Projections and Funding Strategies

Financial projections and funding strategies are integral components of a comprehensive business plan, providing a roadmap for your business's financial trajectory and outlining how you plan to secure the necessary capital to fuel your venture. Let's delve into these key elements:

1. **Financial Projections:**
- **Revenue Forecasting:** Predicting your business's income based on sales projections, pricing strategies, and market demand.
- **Expense Projections:** Estimating your operating costs, including fixed and variable expenses, to determine your net profit.
- **Cash Flow Statement:** Illustrating how changes in your balance sheet and income statements affect cash and cash equivalents over a specific period.

Financial projections offer a glimpse into the future financial health of your business. When creating these projections, it's essential to be realistic, taking into account industry benchmarks, market trends, and potential challenges. Investors and stakeholders often scrutinize financial projections to assess the feasibility and profitability of the business.

2. **Funding Strategies:**

- **Bootstrapping:** Self-funding by using personal savings or revenue generated by the business.
- **Debt Financing:** Obtaining loans or credit from financial institutions, often with interest.
- **Equity Financing:** Securing capital by selling ownership shares in the business to investors.
- **Crowdfunding:** Raising funds from a large number of individuals, typically through online platforms.
- **Angel Investors and Venture Capital:** Attracting investment from high-net-worth individuals (angels) or venture capital firms in exchange for equity.

Choosing the right funding strategy depends on your business's stage, industry, and capital requirements. A combination of funding sources is often employed to mitigate risks and ensure a diverse capital structure.

In "Venture Ignition," the chapter on financial projections and funding strategies guides you through the process of creating realistic financial forecasts and developing a funding plan that aligns with your business goals. Understanding your financial needs and having a clear strategy for obtaining funding enhances your credibility and positions your business for sustainable growth.

Chapter Four
Legal and Regulatory Considerations

Navigating legal and regulatory considerations is a critical aspect of building a strong foundation for your business. Addressing these factors ensures compliance, reduces risks, and establishes a framework that contributes to the long-term success of your venture. Here are key elements to consider:

1. **Business Structure:**
- Choose a legal structure that aligns with your business goals. Options include sole proprietorship, partnership, limited liability company (LLC), corporation, and others. Each structure has implications for taxation, liability, and operational flexibility.

2. **Registration and Licensing:**
- Register your business with the appropriate authorities to operate legally. Obtain the necessary licenses and permits, which vary based on location, industry, and business activities. Compliance with local, state, and federal regulations is crucial.

3. **Intellectual Property Protection:**
- Identify and protect your intellectual property, including trademarks, copyrights, and patents. This

safeguards your unique brand elements, products, or
innovations from infringement.

4. **Contracts and Agreements:**
- Draft clear and comprehensive contracts for business
transactions, partnerships, employment, and client
relationships. Well-drafted agreements can prevent
disputes and provide a legal framework for your business
relationships.

5. **Employment Laws:**
- Familiarize yourself with labor laws and regulations
governing employment relationships. This includes fair
employment practices, wage and hour laws, and
workplace safety standards.

6. **Data Protection and Privacy:**
- Understand and comply with data protection and
privacy laws. Safeguarding customer and employee
information is essential, especially with the increasing
focus on data privacy.

7. **Tax Compliance:**
- Comply with tax regulations at the local, state, and
federal levels. Understand your tax obligations, keep
accurate financial records, and meet filing deadlines to
avoid penalties.

8. **Environmental Regulations:**
- If applicable to your industry, be aware of and adhere to environmental regulations. This is particularly important for businesses involved in manufacturing, construction, or other activities with potential environmental impact.

In "Venture Ignition," the chapter on legal and regulatory considerations provides detailed guidance on navigating these complex aspects. Understanding and proactively addressing legal and regulatory requirements not only protects your business but also fosters trust among customers, partners, and investors. Regular updates on changes in laws or regulations relevant to your industry are crucial to maintaining compliance and adapting to evolving legal landscapes.

4.1 Choosing the Right Business Structure

Choosing the right business structure is a pivotal decision that profoundly impacts your business's legal and financial aspects. Each structure comes with its own set of advantages, disadvantages, and implications for taxation, liability, and operational flexibility. Here are common business structures to consider:

1. **Sole Proprietorship:**

- **Advantages:** Simple to set up, full control, and minimal regulatory requirements.
- **Disadvantages:** Unlimited personal liability, limited access to capital, and potential challenges in business continuity.

2. **Partnership:**
- **Advantages:** Shared responsibilities, pooled resources, and potential for diversified skills.
- **Disadvantages:** Shared profits, potential for disputes between partners, and personal liability for general partners.

3. **Limited Liability Company (LLC):**
- **Advantages:** Limited liability for owners, flexibility in management, and pass-through taxation.
- **Disadvantages:** Some administrative requirements, and regulations may vary by state.

4. **Corporation:**
- **Advantages:** Limited liability for shareholders, ability to raise capital through stock issuance, and continuity of existence.
- **Disadvantages:** Complex regulatory requirements, potential double taxation, and more formalities in operation.

5. **S Corporation:**

- **Advantages:** Pass-through taxation, limited liability for shareholders, and avoidance of double taxation.
- **Disadvantages:** Restrictions on ownership, eligibility criteria, and additional formalities.

6. **Nonprofit Organization:**
- **Advantages:** Tax-exempt status, ability to seek grants and donations, and a focus on a mission or cause.
- **Disadvantages:** Limited profit distribution, strict regulatory oversight, and compliance with nonprofit regulations.

When selecting a business structure, consider factors such as the nature of your business, your long-term goals, the level of control you desire, and the potential tax implications. It's advisable to consult with legal and financial professionals to ensure you make an informed decision aligned with your business objectives.

In "Venture Ignition," the chapter on choosing the right business structure provides detailed insights and considerations to help you navigate this crucial decision. Understanding the implications of each structure empowers you to make a choice that aligns with your business vision and sets the stage for long-term success.

4.2 Navigating Licensing and Compliance

Navigating licensing and compliance is a crucial aspect of running a business, ensuring that your operations adhere to legal requirements and industry regulations. Failing to comply with licensing and regulatory standards can lead to penalties, legal issues, and damage to your business reputation. Here's a guide on navigating licensing and compliance:

1. **Identify Applicable Licenses:**
- Research and identify the specific licenses and permits required for your business at the local, state, and federal levels. The types of licenses vary based on the nature of your business, location, and industry.

2. **Understand Industry Regulations:**
- Familiarize yourself with industry-specific regulations governing your business. Different sectors may have unique compliance requirements, such as health and safety standards, environmental regulations, or financial regulations.

3. **Application Process:**
- Follow the prescribed application process for obtaining the necessary licenses. This may involve submitting documentation, paying fees, and meeting specific criteria. Begin this process well in advance to avoid delays in launching or operating your business.

4. **Renewal and Updates:**
- Stay vigilant about license renewals and updates. Licensing requirements may change over time, and ensuring that your business stays in compliance is an ongoing responsibility. Keep accurate records of renewal deadlines.

5. **Compliance with Zoning Laws:**
- Check and comply with zoning laws that regulate the use of land and property. Zoning regulations dictate where specific types of businesses can operate and may impact your location choice.

6. **Employee Regulations:**
- Adhere to employment laws and regulations, including fair labor practices, minimum wage laws, and workplace safety standards. Maintaining compliance in these areas fosters a healthy and legal work environment.

7. **Record-Keeping:**
- Establish robust record-keeping practices to track licenses, permits, and compliance documentation. This documentation may be required during audits or inspections.

8. **Seek Legal Advice:**

- Consult with legal professionals or specialists in your industry to ensure that you fully understand and comply with all relevant licensing and regulatory requirements. Legal guidance can help you navigate complex regulations and mitigate risks.

In "Venture Ignition," the chapter on licensing and compliance provides comprehensive insights and practical tips to help you navigate this complex terrain. Understanding and proactively addressing licensing and compliance issues are essential for the smooth and legal operation of your business, contributing to its overall success and sustainability.

Chapter Five
Building Your Brand

Building your brand is a multifaceted process that goes beyond creating a logo. It involves shaping the perception of your business, establishing a unique identity, and fostering connections with your target audience. Here are key considerations when building your brand:

1. **Define Your Brand Identity:**
- Clarify your mission, vision, and values. Your brand identity should reflect who you are, what you stand for, and the unique qualities that set your business apart.

2. **Create a Memorable Logo and Visual Elements:**
- Design a distinctive logo and visual elements that resonate with your brand identity. Consistency in colors, fonts, and imagery helps create a cohesive and recognizable brand image.

3. **Craft a Unique Value Proposition (UVP):**
- Clearly articulate what makes your products or services unique and valuable. Your UVP should address the specific needs and desires of your target audience.

4. **Understand Your Target Audience:**
- Conduct market research to understand the demographics, preferences, and behaviors of your target audience. Tailor your brand messaging to resonate with their interests and values.

5. **Develop Consistent Brand Messaging:**

- Ensure that your messaging, both online and offline, communicates a consistent brand story. From your website content to social media posts, maintain a unified brand voice.

6. **Build an Online Presence:**
- Establish a strong online presence through a user-friendly website and active engagement on social media platforms. Consistent and authentic communication enhances your brand's visibility and accessibility.

7. **Customer Experience:**
- Prioritize a positive customer experience at every touchpoint. From the first interaction to post-purchase support, each interaction contributes to your brand's reputation.

8. **Brand Consistency Across Platforms:**
- Maintain consistency in branding across various platforms and channels. Whether it's your website, social media, or physical storefront, a cohesive brand presentation reinforces brand recognition.

9. **Engage in Storytelling:**
- Share compelling stories about your brand's journey, values, and impact. Authentic storytelling fosters emotional connections with your audience.

10. **Collect and Respond to Feedback:**
- Actively seek and respond to customer feedback. Addressing concerns and showcasing positive experiences demonstrates your commitment to customer satisfaction.

11. **Adapt and Evolve:**
- Brands evolve over time. Stay attuned to market trends, customer preferences, and industry changes. Adapt your brand strategy to remain relevant and competitive.

In "Venture Ignition," the chapter on building your brand provides detailed insights and actionable steps to guide you through the brand-building process. By investing in a strong and authentic brand, you create a lasting impression that resonates with your audience and contributes to the overall success of your business.

5.1 Creating a Unique Value Proposition

Creating a unique value proposition (UVP) is a strategic process that articulates the specific benefits and value your business provides to customers. A compelling UVP sets your brand apart, attracts your target audience, and forms the foundation of your marketing messages. Here's a guide to creating a unique value proposition:

1. **Understand Customer Needs:**
- Conduct thorough market research to identify the needs, challenges, and desires of your target audience. Understanding your customers is essential for crafting a UVP that resonates with them.

2. **Identify Your Differentiators:**
- Pinpoint the unique aspects of your products, services, or brand that distinguish you from competitors. This could include features, quality, pricing, or a specific niche focus.

3. **Highlight Key Benefits:**
- Clearly articulate the primary benefits customers gain by choosing your business. Focus on how your offerings solve problems, fulfill needs, or provide value that competitors may not offer.

4. **Be Clear and Concise:**
- Keep your UVP succinct and easy to understand. Avoid jargon and communicate the essence of your value proposition in a brief and compelling manner.

5. **Emphasize Emotional Appeal:**
- Appeal to emotions by highlighting how your brand makes customers feel or how it aligns with their values. Emotional connections often play a significant role in purchasing decisions.

6. **Address Pain Points:**
- Demonstrate an understanding of customer pain points and position your UVP as a solution. Showing that your business can alleviate challenges builds trust and credibility.

7. **Quantify Benefits When Possible:**
- Whenever feasible, quantify the benefits of your offerings. Whether it's saving time, reducing costs, or improving efficiency, providing specific numbers adds credibility to your UVP.

8. **Test and Refine:**
- Test your UVP with your target audience to gauge its effectiveness. Gather feedback and be open to refining your value proposition based on customer insights.

9. **Align with Brand Identity:**
- Ensure that your UVP aligns with your overall brand identity. Consistency in messaging and branding reinforces your value proposition and builds a cohesive brand image.

10. **Monitor Competitor UVPs:**
- Stay informed about your competitors' value propositions. This helps you identify opportunities to

differentiate and ensures that your UVP remains distinctive in the market.

11. **Highlight Your USP (Unique Selling Proposition):**
- Clearly communicate what makes your business uniquely positioned to fulfill customer needs. Whether it's innovation, expertise, or a specific approach, emphasize your USP in your UVP.

By investing time and thought into creating a compelling unique value proposition, you set the stage for effective marketing, customer acquisition, and long-term brand loyalty. In "Venture Ignition," the chapter on creating a unique value proposition offers detailed guidance and practical tips to help you refine this essential aspect of your business strategy.

5.2 Effective Branding Strategies for Startups

Effective branding is crucial for startups to establish a strong presence, build credibility, and connect with their target audience. Here are key branding strategies tailored for startups:

1. **Define Your Brand Identity:**

- Clearly articulate your mission, vision, and values. This foundation forms the basis of your brand identity and guides all branding efforts.

2. **Create a Distinctive Logo and Visual Elements:**
   - Design a memorable logo and consistent visual elements that reflect your brand identity. Visual cohesion enhances brand recognition.

3. **Craft a Compelling Unique Value Proposition (UVP):**
- Develop a UVP that clearly communicates the unique benefits your startup provides. Focus on what sets you apart from competitors.

4. **Leverage Storytelling:**
- Share your startup story authentically. Highlight the journey, challenges overcome, and the passion driving your venture. Storytelling fosters emotional connections with your audience.

5. **Build a Strong Online Presence:**
- Establish a user-friendly website and active presence on relevant social media platforms. Utilize content marketing to showcase your expertise and engage with your audience.

6. **Engage in Social Responsibility:**

- Demonstrate a commitment to social responsibility. Participate in community initiatives or support causes aligned with your brand values. This enhances your brand's reputation.

7. **Create Consistent Brand Messaging:**
- Maintain a consistent brand voice across all communication channels. Whether on your website, social media, or marketing materials, a unified message reinforces brand identity.

8. **Offer Exceptional Customer Experience:**
- Prioritize customer satisfaction. Deliver exceptional products or services, and ensure positive interactions at every touchpoint. Happy customers become brand advocates.

9. **Utilize Influencer Marketing:**
- Collaborate with influencers or thought leaders in your industry. Their endorsement can amplify your brand's reach and credibility, especially in the early stages.

10. **Encourage User-Generated Content:**
- Encourage customers to share their experiences with your brand. User-generated content on social media serves as authentic testimonials and boosts brand authenticity.

11. **Participate in Industry Events:**
- Attend and actively participate in industry events, conferences, and trade shows. Networking and showcasing your startup at relevant events enhance industry visibility.

12. **Adaptability and Agility:**
- Be adaptable and agile in response to market feedback and changes. A startup's ability to pivot and evolve is a strength that resonates positively with audiences.

13. **Focus on Brand Consistency:**
- Consistency across all branding elements is key. From visuals to messaging and customer interactions, a cohesive brand presentation builds trust.

14. **Monitor Analytics and Iterate:**
- Use analytics to track the effectiveness of your branding strategies. Analyze data, gather feedback, and iterate on your branding efforts to optimize results.

In "Venture Ignition," the chapter on effective branding strategies for startups offers detailed insights and practical tips to guide startups through the process of building a strong and resonant brand. Implementing these strategies strategically can contribute to the success and sustainability of your startup.

Chapter Six
Setting Up Operations

Setting up operations is a crucial phase for startups, requiring careful planning and execution. Efficient operations lay the groundwork for delivering products or services, managing resources, and meeting customer expectations. Here are key steps to consider when setting up operations for your startup:

1. **Establish Clear Processes:**
- Define and document your core business processes. Clearly outline how tasks are executed, roles and responsibilities, and the flow of information within your startup.

2. **Select an Appropriate Location:**
- Choose a location that aligns with your business needs. Consider factors such as proximity to suppliers, target market, and cost of operation.

3. **Build a Strong Team:**
- Recruit skilled and dedicated team members. Ensure each member understands their role, and foster a collaborative and positive work culture.

4. **Invest in Technology:**
- Implement technology solutions that streamline operations. This may include project management tools, communication platforms, and software for financial management.

5. **Supply Chain Management:**
- Establish a reliable supply chain. Identify and partner with trustworthy suppliers to ensure a steady flow of materials or resources needed for your products or services.

6. **Inventory Management:**
- Implement efficient inventory management systems. Monitor stock levels, track product movement, and optimize inventory to avoid overstocking or stockouts.

7. **Quality Control Measures:**
- Develop and implement quality control measures to ensure consistency and excellence in your products or services. Regularly assess and refine these measures as needed.

8. **Customer Support Systems:**
- Set up effective customer support systems. This includes clear communication channels, trained support staff, and mechanisms for gathering and addressing customer feedback.

9. **Compliance with Regulations:**
- Ensure compliance with industry regulations and standards. Stay informed about any legal requirements that impact your operations and make adjustments accordingly.

10. **Risk Management:**
- Identify potential risks to your operations and develop risk management strategies. This may involve contingency plans for disruptions, financial risk assessments, and cybersecurity measures.

11. **Financial Management:**
- Establish robust financial management practices. Implement accounting systems, budgeting processes, and

financial reporting to maintain financial health and transparency.

12. **Scalability Considerations:**
- Design your operations with scalability in mind. Anticipate future growth and ensure that your operations can adapt to increased demand and expansion.

13. **Training and Development:**
- Invest in training and development programs for your team. Continuous learning ensures that your team stays skilled and informed about industry trends.

14. **Environmental Sustainability:**
- Consider environmentally sustainable practices in your operations. This not only aligns with modern values but can also lead to cost savings and positive brand perception.

In "Venture Ignition," the chapter on setting up operations provides comprehensive insights and practical guidance to help startups navigate the complexities of establishing efficient and effective operations. Careful planning and attention to these operational aspects contribute significantly to the overall success of your startup.

6.1 Location and Infrastructure

Choosing the right location and establishing robust infrastructure are pivotal decisions for startups, influencing accessibility, cost-effectiveness, and overall operational efficiency. Here are key considerations for both aspects:

Location:

1. **Proximity to Target Market:**
- Select a location that is easily accessible to your target market. Understanding your customer demographics can help pinpoint an area that aligns with your business strategy.

2. **Cost of Operation:**
- Evaluate the overall cost of operating in a specific location, including rent, utilities, and taxes. Striking a balance between cost and benefits is crucial for startup sustainability.

3. **Competitive Landscape:**
- Research the competitive landscape in potential locations. Consider whether being close to competitors is advantageous or if finding a niche in a less saturated area is more strategic.

4. **Infrastructure and Amenities:**

- Assess the local infrastructure and amenities
available. Consider factors such as transportation, access
to utilities, and nearby services that can impact your
daily operations.

5. **Regulatory Environment:**
- Understand the regulatory environment of the chosen
location. Be aware of zoning laws, business regulations,
and any industry-specific requirements that may affect
your operations.

6. **Talent Pool:**
- Consider the availability of a skilled workforce in the
area. Access to a relevant talent pool can significantly
impact your ability to recruit and retain key team
members.

7. **Networking Opportunities:**
- Evaluate the networking opportunities in the chosen
location. Being in proximity to industry events,
networking groups, and potential partners can enhance
your business connections.

Infrastructure:

1. **Technology and Connectivity:**
- Ensure that the chosen location has reliable
technology infrastructure and connectivity. High-speed

internet and access to digital resources are critical for modern businesses.

2. **Office Space and Facilities:**
- Secure suitable office space with the necessary facilities to support your operations. Consider factors such as meeting rooms, collaborative spaces, and amenities for your team.

3. **Security Measures:**
- Implement robust security measures for your physical and digital assets. This includes securing your office space, data, and any sensitive information.

4. **Scalability Planning:**
- Plan for scalability in your infrastructure. Anticipate growth and ensure that your chosen facilities can accommodate an expanding team and increased operational needs.

5. **Environmental Considerations:**
- Consider environmental factors such as energy efficiency and sustainability in your infrastructure choices. Green practices not only align with modern values but can also result in cost savings.

6. **Backup and Redundancy:**

- Establish backup and redundancy systems for critical operations. This includes data backup, alternative power sources, and contingency plans for potential disruptions.

7. **Compliance with Safety Standards:**
- Ensure that your infrastructure complies with safety standards and regulations. This may involve fire safety measures, ergonomic considerations, and adherence to building codes.

In "Venture Ignition," the chapter on location and infrastructure provides detailed insights and practical guidance to help startups make informed decisions when selecting a location and establishing the necessary infrastructure for their operations. Careful consideration of these factors contributes to the overall efficiency and success of your startup.

6.2 Supply Chain and Inventory Management

Effectively managing your supply chain and inventory is critical for ensuring a smooth flow of products or services and maintaining customer satisfaction. Here are key considerations for supply chain and inventory management:

Supply Chain Management:

1. **Supplier Relationships:**
- Cultivate strong relationships with reliable suppliers. Clear communication and collaboration enhance the efficiency of your supply chain.

2. **Diversification of Suppliers:**
- Consider diversifying your sources of supply to mitigate risks. Depending on a single supplier may expose your business to disruptions.

3. **Demand Forecasting:**
- Utilize data and market insights for accurate demand forecasting. Understanding future demand helps optimize inventory levels and production schedules.

4. **Lead Time Reduction:**
- Work on reducing lead times in your supply chain. This minimizes delays and allows for more agile responses to changes in demand.

5. **Quality Control:**
- Implement stringent quality control measures. Ensuring the quality of incoming materials or components is crucial for maintaining the integrity of your products.

6. **Risk Management:**

- Identify potential risks in your supply chain and develop risk mitigation strategies. This may include having backup suppliers or alternative sourcing options.

7. **Technology Integration:**
- Utilize technology for supply chain visibility and coordination. Technologies such as RFID, IoT, and supply chain management software enhance efficiency and accuracy.

8. **Sustainability Practices:**
- Consider sustainability practices in your supply chain. This not only aligns with environmental values but can also positively impact your brand.

Inventory Management:

1. **ABC Analysis:**
- Classify your inventory into categories (A, B, C) based on importance. This helps prioritize attention and resources on high-value items.

2. **Safety Stock:**
- Maintain safety stock to buffer against unexpected demand spikes or supply chain disruptions. This ensures you can fulfill orders even in challenging circumstances.

3. **Just-In-Time (JIT) Inventory:**

- Consider JIT inventory management for items with predictable demand. This strategy minimizes carrying costs by ordering goods only when needed.

4. **Regular Audits:**
- Conduct regular audits to track inventory accuracy. Implement cycle counting or periodic checks to identify discrepancies and avoid stockouts or overstocking.

5. **Supplier Collaboration:**
- Collaborate with suppliers to implement vendor-managed inventory (VMI) systems. This allows suppliers to manage and replenish your inventory based on agreed-upon levels.

6. **Integrated Systems:**
- Integrate inventory management systems with other business processes. This ensures real-time data sharing and reduces the likelihood of errors.

7. **Order Fulfillment Optimization:**
- Optimize order fulfillment processes. Efficient picking, packing, and shipping contribute to faster delivery times and enhanced customer satisfaction.

8. **Technology Adoption:**
- Leverage technology such as inventory management software and barcode systems. Automation improves

accuracy and efficiency in tracking and managing inventory.

In "Venture Ignition," the chapter on supply chain and inventory management provides detailed insights and practical tips to help startups streamline their operations. Implementing effective supply chain and inventory management practices is essential for meeting customer demands, minimizing costs, and achieving overall business success.

Chapter Seven
Marketing and Sales

Marketing and sales are integral components of a startup's success, driving customer acquisition, revenue generation, and brand awareness. Here are key considerations for effective marketing and sales strategies:

Marketing:

1. **Define Your Target Audience:**
- Clearly identify and understand your target audience.
Tailor your marketing strategies to resonate with the
demographics, preferences, and behaviors of your ideal
customers.

2. **Craft a Compelling Value Proposition:**
- Develop a unique value proposition that
communicates the benefits of your products or services.
Clearly articulate what sets your offerings apart from
competitors.

3. **Utilize Digital Marketing Channels:**
- Leverage digital marketing channels such as social
media, search engine optimization (SEO), email
marketing, and content marketing. Choose platforms that
align with your target audience.

4. **Content Marketing:**
- Create valuable and relevant content that educates,
entertains, or solves problems for your audience. Content
marketing establishes your authority in the industry and
attracts potential customers.

5. **Brand Consistency:**

- Maintain consistency in your brand messaging and visuals across all marketing channels. A cohesive brand presentation builds trust and recognition.

6. **Influencer Collaborations:**
- Explore collaborations with influencers or thought leaders in your industry. Their endorsement can extend your reach and credibility.

7. **Customer Testimonials:**
- Showcase customer testimonials and success stories. Positive reviews and testimonials provide social proof and build confidence in your brand.

8. **Data Analytics:**
- Utilize data analytics to measure the effectiveness of your marketing efforts. Monitor key performance indicators (KPIs) to understand what strategies are working and where adjustments are needed.

Sales:

1. **Build a Sales Team:**
- Assemble a skilled and motivated sales team. Provide training, clear goals, and incentives to drive performance.

2. **Customer Relationship Management (CRM):**

- Implement a CRM system to manage customer interactions, track leads, and streamline the sales process. A well-organized CRM enhances customer relationships.

3. **Sales Funnel Optimization:**
- Optimize your sales funnel to guide leads through the stages of awareness, consideration, and decision-making. Ensure a smooth and engaging customer journey.

4. **Effective Communication:**
- Train your sales team in effective communication and active listening. Understanding customer needs allows for personalized and persuasive sales pitches.

5. **Sales Enablement Tools:**
- Provide your sales team with tools and resources that facilitate their work. This may include sales playbooks, email templates, and product knowledge resources.

6. **Upselling and Cross-Selling Strategies:**
- Implement strategies for upselling and cross-selling to maximize revenue from existing customers. Offer complementary products or upgrades based on their needs.

7. **Sales Metrics Tracking:**

- Monitor key sales metrics such as conversion rates, average deal size, and sales cycle length. Regularly analyze these metrics to identify areas for improvement.

8. **Continuous Training:**
- Invest in ongoing training for your sales team. Stay updated on industry trends, product updates, and sales techniques to maintain a competitive edge.

In "Venture Ignition," the chapters on marketing and sales provide comprehensive insights and actionable strategies to guide startups in effectively promoting their products or services and driving revenue growth. Successful integration of marketing and sales efforts contributes to a robust and sustainable business model.

7.1 Developing a Marketing Plan

Developing a comprehensive marketing plan is essential for startups to outline strategies, goals, and tactics for promoting their products or services. Here's a structured guide to help you create an effective marketing plan:

Executive Summary:

1. **Business Overview:**
- Provide a brief overview of your startup, its mission, and the products or services you offer.

2. **Key Objectives:**
- Clearly define your marketing objectives. These could include increasing brand awareness, driving sales, or expanding into new markets.

Situation Analysis:

3. **Market Analysis:**
- Analyze your target market. Identify demographics, behaviors, and trends that impact your industry.

4. **Competitor Analysis:**
- Evaluate your competitors. Understand their strengths, weaknesses, and market positioning.

5. **SWOT Analysis:**
- Conduct a SWOT analysis (Strengths, Weaknesses, Opportunities, Threats) for your startup. This helps identify internal and external factors affecting your marketing strategy.

Target Audience:

6. **Customer Segmentation:**
- Define your target audience segments. Consider factors like age, location, interests, and purchasing behavior.

7. **Buyer Personas:**
- Create detailed buyer personas for your ideal customers. This helps tailor your marketing messages more effectively.

Marketing Strategies:

8. **Positioning Strategy:**
- Clearly articulate your brand positioning. Highlight what makes your startup unique in the market.

9. **Value Proposition:**
- Refine and communicate your unique value proposition. Clearly state the benefits customers gain from choosing your products or services.

10. **Channel Selection:**
- Choose the marketing channels that align with your target audience. This could include social media, content marketing, email, or traditional advertising.

11. **Content Strategy:**
- Develop a content strategy. Plan the types of content you'll create, the platforms you'll use, and the schedule for distribution.

Tactics and Implementation:

12. **Campaign Calendar:**
- Create a detailed calendar outlining your marketing campaigns. Include launch dates, milestones, and key promotional periods.

13. **Budget Allocation:**
- Allocate your marketing budget across different channels and tactics. Ensure a balanced approach that aligns with your objectives.

14. **Partnerships and Collaborations:**
- Explore partnerships or collaborations with influencers, other businesses, or organizations that can amplify your reach.

Measurement and Analytics:

15. **Key Performance Indicators (KPIs):**
- Define the KPIs that align with your objectives. This could include website traffic, conversion rates, social media engagement, or sales metrics.

16. **Analytics Tools:**
- Implement analytics tools to track and measure your KPIs. This may include Google Analytics, social media insights, or specific marketing automation platforms.

17. **Regular Evaluation:**
- Schedule regular evaluations to assess the performance of your marketing strategies. Use the data to refine and adjust your approach.

Conclusion and Future Plans:

18. **Conclusion:**
- Summarize the key points of your marketing plan. Emphasize the strategies you believe will be most impactful.

19. **Future Plans:**
- Outline future plans and adjustments based on the insights gained from ongoing evaluations. Consider how you'll adapt to changes in the market or your business environment.

In "Venture Ignition," the chapter on developing a marketing plan provides detailed guidance and practical tips to help you create a tailored and effective marketing strategy for your startup.

7.2 Sales Strategies for New Businesses

Implementing effective sales strategies is crucial for new businesses to acquire customers and drive revenue. Here are key sales strategies tailored for startups:

1. **Understand Your Ideal Customer:**
- Clearly define your target audience and understand their needs, pain points, and preferences. Tailor your sales approach to resonate with your ideal customer.

2. **Build Relationships:**
- Focus on building genuine relationships with potential customers. Establish trust and credibility, as this can be a key differentiator for a new business.

3. **Provide Value:**
- Emphasize the value your product or service provides. Clearly articulate how it solves problems or fulfills needs for your customers.

4. **Leverage Digital Marketing:**
- Use digital marketing strategies to generate leads and create brand awareness. This includes social media marketing, content marketing, and search engine optimization.

5. **Utilize Inbound Marketing:**
- Implement inbound marketing techniques to attract leads organically. Create valuable content that addresses customer needs and positions your startup as an authority in the industry.

6. **Effective Networking:**
- Attend industry events, join business networks, and engage in online communities relevant to your niche. Networking helps you connect with potential customers and build partnerships.

7. **Offer Limited-Time Promotions:**
- Introduce limited-time promotions or early bird offers to incentivize early adoption. This creates a sense of urgency and encourages customers to make a purchasing decision.

8. **Referral Programs:**
- Establish referral programs that encourage satisfied customers to refer others. Word-of-mouth marketing is powerful, especially for new businesses.

9. **Sales Funnel Optimization:**
- Optimize your sales funnel to guide potential customers through the stages of awareness, consideration, and decision-making. Ensure a smooth and engaging customer journey.

10. **Product Demonstrations:**
- Conduct product demonstrations to showcase the features and benefits of your offerings. This can be particularly effective for products or services that benefit from hands-on experience.

11. **Leverage Testimonials:**
- Collect and showcase customer testimonials. Positive reviews and testimonials build credibility and provide social proof to potential customers.

12. **Flexible Pricing Options:**
- Offer flexible pricing options, such as discounts for annual subscriptions or customizable packages. This gives customers choices that suit their budgets and preferences.

13. **Sales Training:**
- Invest in training for your sales team. Ensure they have a deep understanding of your products or services, effective communication skills, and the ability to address customer objections.

14. **Utilize Sales Technologies:**
- Implement sales technologies, such as customer relationship management (CRM) systems and sales automation tools, to streamline processes and enhance efficiency.

15. **Customer Education:**
- Educate potential customers about your industry, product, or service. Provide valuable insights through

webinars, tutorials, or informative content to position your startup as an authority.

16. **Adaptability:**
- Be adaptable to customer feedback and market changes. Adjust your sales strategies based on insights gained from customer interactions and market dynamics.

In "Venture Ignition," the chapter on sales strategies for new businesses offers detailed insights and practical tips to guide startups in building effective and sustainable sales approaches. Implementing a combination of these strategies can contribute to the successful growth of your startup.

Chapter Eight
Financial Management

Effective financial management is crucial for the success and sustainability of any startup. Here are key considerations for managing the financial aspects of your business:

Budgeting:

1. **Create a Detailed Budget:**
- Develop a comprehensive budget that includes all expenses, from operational costs to marketing and personnel. Regularly review and adjust the budget as needed.

2. **Prioritize Spending:**
- Prioritize spending based on critical business needs. Allocate resources to areas that directly contribute to revenue generation and core operations.

3. **Emergency Fund:**
- Establish an emergency fund to cover unexpected expenses or address temporary cash flow challenges. This buffer provides financial stability during uncertain times.

Financial Planning:

4. **Set Financial Goals:**
- Define clear financial goals for your startup. These goals may include revenue targets, profit margins, and milestones for growth.

5. **Cash Flow Management:**
- Monitor and manage your cash flow effectively.
Ensure that you have enough cash on hand to cover
operational expenses and invest in growth opportunities.

6. **Forecasting:**
- Implement financial forecasting to anticipate future
financial needs and challenges. This allows you to
proactively address potential issues and plan for growth.

Accounting and Record-Keeping:

7. **Use Reliable Accounting Software:**
- Invest in reliable accounting software to streamline
financial processes. This helps maintain accurate records
and facilitates easy reporting.

8. **Regular Financial Audits:**
- Conduct regular financial audits to review your
financial statements and ensure accuracy. Audits also
identify areas for improvement and potential cost
savings.

Funding and Capital:

9. **Explore Funding Options:**

- Explore different funding options, including equity financing, loans, or grants. Choose the option that aligns with your business goals and financial needs.

10. **Investment Decisions:**
- Make informed investment decisions. Assess the potential return on investment (ROI) and weigh the benefits against the costs before committing to any significant expenditures.

Financial Controls:

11. **Implement Internal Controls:**
- Establish internal controls to prevent fraud and ensure the accuracy of financial reporting. This includes segregation of duties and regular review processes.

12. **Expense Management:**
- Implement strict expense management policies. Require approvals for significant expenses and regularly review spending patterns to identify cost-saving opportunities.

Tax Planning:

13. **Compliance with Tax Regulations:**

- Ensure compliance with tax regulations at the local, state, and federal levels. Stay informed about tax incentives and deductions applicable to your business.

14. **Tax Planning Strategies:**
- Develop tax planning strategies to minimize tax liabilities. Consult with tax professionals to optimize your financial position.

Continuous Monitoring and Adjustment:

15. **Key Performance Indicators (KPIs):**
- Identify and monitor key financial performance indicators. Regularly assess metrics such as profitability, liquidity, and efficiency.

16. **Adapt to Market Changes:**
- Stay agile and adapt your financial strategies to changes in the market, industry trends, and economic conditions. Flexibility is crucial for long-term financial sustainability.

In "Venture Ignition," the chapter on financial management provides detailed insights and practical guidance to help startups navigate the complexities of financial planning and execution. By implementing sound financial practices, startups can enhance their resilience and position themselves for long-term success.

8.1 Budgeting and Financial Control

Budgeting and financial control are essential components of effective financial management for startups. Here's a guide to help you establish a robust budget and implement financial controls:

Budgeting:

1. **Define Financial Goals:**
- Clearly define your financial goals, whether it's achieving profitability, increasing revenue, or managing costs. Your budget should align with these overarching objectives.

2. **Create a Detailed Budget:**
- Develop a comprehensive budget that covers all aspects of your business, including operational expenses, marketing, personnel, and any planned investments. Break down the budget into monthly or quarterly segments.

3. **Sales Forecasting:**
- Base your budget on realistic sales forecasts. Consider market trends, historical data, and any factors that may impact sales, such as seasonality.

4. **Expense Categories:**
- Categorize expenses into fixed and variable categories. Fixed costs remain consistent, while variable costs fluctuate with business activity. This distinction helps in better cost management.

5. **Emergency Fund Allocation:**
- Allocate a portion of your budget to an emergency fund. This fund serves as a financial buffer to cover unexpected expenses or navigate challenging periods.

6. **Regular Budget Reviews:**
- Conduct regular reviews of your budget. Compare actual expenses and revenues against your budgeted figures, and make adjustments as necessary. This ongoing evaluation ensures your budget remains aligned with business realities.

Financial Control:

7. **Internal Controls:**
- Implement internal controls to safeguard against fraud and errors. Clearly define roles and responsibilities, segregate duties, and conduct regular internal audits.

8. **Approval Processes:**

- Establish approval processes for significant expenses. Having a system in place where key expenditures require approval helps maintain financial discipline.

9. **Expense Management Policies:**
- Develop and communicate clear expense management policies. This includes guidelines on spending limits, approval procedures, and documentation requirements for reimbursements.

10. **Regular Financial Reports:**
- Generate regular financial reports, including income statements, balance sheets, and cash flow statements. These reports provide insights into your financial health and aid in decision-making.

11. **Key Performance Indicators (KPIs):**
- Define and monitor key financial performance indicators (KPIs) relevant to your business. Common financial KPIs include gross margin, net profit margin, and return on investment (ROI).

12. **Cash Flow Monitoring:**
- Keep a close eye on your cash flow. Maintain a cash flow statement to track the movement of cash in and out of your business. Address any cash flow challenges promptly.

13. **Variance Analysis:**
- Conduct variance analysis to compare actual financial results with budgeted figures. Understand the reasons for any variances and adjust your strategies accordingly.

14. **Regular Financial Audits:**
- Conduct regular financial audits, either internally or externally. Audits provide an independent assessment of your financial processes and help ensure compliance.

15. **Financial Training for Team Members:**
- Provide financial training for relevant team members. Ensure that key personnel understand budgetary constraints, financial goals, and the importance of financial control.

16. **Continuous Improvement:**
- Foster a culture of continuous improvement in financial management. Encourage feedback, learn from past experiences, and adapt your financial control measures to evolving business needs.

In "Venture Ignition," the chapter on budgeting and financial control provides detailed insights and practical guidance to help startups establish effective financial frameworks. Implementing robust budgeting and

financial control practices contributes to financial
stability and positions your startup for long-term success.

8.2 Accounting and Bookkeeping Essentials

Accounting and bookkeeping are foundational elements
for startups to maintain financial transparency, comply
with regulations, and make informed business decisions.
Here's a guide to the essentials of accounting and
bookkeeping:

Bookkeeping Basics:

1. **Chart of Accounts:**
- Establish a chart of accounts that categorizes your
financial transactions. Common categories include
assets, liabilities, equity, revenue, and expenses.

2. **Double-Entry System:**
- Follow the double-entry system, where every
transaction has equal and opposite effects on at least two
accounts. This system ensures accurate recording of
financial activities.

3. **Record Financial Transactions:**
- Record all financial transactions systematically. This
includes sales, purchases, expenses, and any other
financial activities relevant to your business.

4. **Bank Reconciliation:**
- Regularly reconcile your bank statements with your accounting records. This process helps identify discrepancies and ensures accurate financial reporting.

5. **Invoice and Receipt Tracking:**
- Keep a record of all invoices issued and receipts received. This documentation is essential for tracking revenue and managing accounts receivable.

Accounting Principles:

6. **Accrual vs. Cash Accounting:**
- Choose between accrual and cash accounting based on your business needs. Accrual accounting recognizes revenue and expenses when they are earned or incurred, while cash accounting records transactions when cash changes hands.

7. **Consistency:**
- Maintain consistency in your accounting methods and principles. Consistent accounting practices enhance the accuracy and reliability of financial reports.

8. **Materiality:**
- Apply the materiality principle, focusing on significant financial transactions. Materiality helps

determine which transactions are essential to disclose in financial statements.

Financial Statements:

9. **Income Statement:**
   - Prepare an income statement (profit and loss statement) that summarizes your revenue, expenses, and net income over a specific period. This statement provides insights into your profitability.

10. **Balance Sheet:**
   - Create a balance sheet that presents your assets, liabilities, and equity at a specific point in time. The balance sheet provides a snapshot of your business's financial position.

11. **Cash Flow Statement:**
   - Develop a cash flow statement detailing the inflow and outflow of cash during a specific period. This statement is crucial for understanding liquidity and managing cash effectively.

Compliance and Reporting:

12. **Tax Compliance:**
   - Ensure compliance with tax regulations relevant to your business. Keep accurate records, meet filing

deadlines, and take advantage of available tax
deductions.

13. **Financial Reporting:**
- Regularly produce financial reports, including the income statement, balance sheet, and cash flow statement. These reports are essential for internal analysis and external reporting requirements.

14. **Audit Preparation:**
- Maintain organized and accurate records in preparation for potential audits. This includes supporting documentation for financial transactions and adherence to accounting standards.

Accounting Software:

15. **Choose Suitable Accounting Software:**
- Select accounting software that meets your business needs. Popular options include QuickBooks, Xero, and FreshBooks. These tools streamline bookkeeping processes and enhance accuracy.

16. **Automation and Integration:**
- Leverage automation features in accounting software. Automation reduces manual errors and ensures efficiency in recording and reconciling financial transactions.

Professional Guidance:

17. **Consult with an Accountant:**
- Seek guidance from a professional accountant, especially during critical financial decisions or when facing complex transactions. An accountant can provide valuable insights and ensure compliance.

18. **Continuous Learning:**
- Stay informed about changes in accounting standards, tax regulations, and financial reporting requirements. Continuous learning ensures that your accounting practices remain up-to-date.

In "Venture Ignition," the chapter on accounting and bookkeeping essentials offers detailed insights and practical guidance to help startups establish and maintain effective accounting practices. Sound accounting and bookkeeping contribute to the financial health and sustainability of your business.

Chapter Nine
Hiring and Managing Teams

Hiring and managing teams is a critical aspect of building a successful startup. Here's a guide to help you navigate the process:

Hiring Process:

1. **Define Roles and Responsibilities:**
- Clearly define the roles and responsibilities of each position before starting the hiring process. This ensures that you hire individuals with the right skill sets.

2. **Create Compelling Job Descriptions:**
- Craft detailed and compelling job descriptions. Clearly communicate the expectations, qualifications, and benefits associated with each position.

3. **Utilize Multiple Recruitment Channels:**
- Use a variety of recruitment channels, including job boards, social media, and networking events, to reach a diverse pool of candidates.

4. **Streamlined Application Process:**
- Simplify the application process to encourage more qualified candidates to apply. A user-friendly application process enhances the candidate experience.

5. **Thorough Screening:**
- Screen candidates thoroughly, considering their skills, experience, and cultural fit. Initial interviews and assessments can help narrow down the pool.

6. **Behavioral Interviews:**
- Incorporate behavioral interviews to assess how candidates handle real-life situations. This provides insights into their problem-solving skills and cultural alignment.

7. **Reference Checks:**
- Conduct reference checks to verify candidates' work history and performance. Contact previous employers or colleagues to gain additional perspectives.

8. **Cultural Fit Assessment:**
- Assess cultural fit during the interview process. A team that aligns with your startup's values contributes to a positive work environment.

Onboarding:

9. **Structured Onboarding Program:**
- Implement a structured onboarding program for new hires. This program should include an introduction to

company culture, team dynamics, and job-specific training.

10. **Mentorship:**
- Assign mentors to new employees. Having a mentor helps newcomers acclimate to the company culture and understand their roles more effectively.

Team Management:

11. **Set Clear Expectations:**
- Clearly communicate expectations and goals to your team. This fosters accountability and ensures that everyone is aligned with the company's objectives.

12. **Regular Communication:**
- Establish regular communication channels within the team. Regular check-ins, team meetings, and updates help maintain transparency and foster collaboration.

13. **Encourage Feedback:**
- Create an environment where team members feel comfortable providing feedback. Both positive feedback and constructive criticism contribute to continuous improvement.

14. **Professional Development:**

- Support professional development opportunities for your team members. This can include training programs, workshops, or opportunities to attend industry conferences.

15. **Recognition and Rewards:**
- Recognize and reward achievements. Celebrate milestones, both big and small, to motivate and show appreciation for your team's hard work.

16. **Conflict Resolution:**
- Address conflicts promptly and constructively. Open communication and a proactive approach to conflict resolution contribute to a healthy work environment.

17. **Flexibility and Work-Life Balance:**
- Promote flexibility and work-life balance. Understanding the individual needs of your team members contributes to job satisfaction and overall well-being.

Team Building:

18. **Team Building Activities:**
- Organize team-building activities to foster camaraderie. These activities can be both work-related and social to build strong relationships among team members.

19. **Celebrate Diversity:**
- Embrace and celebrate diversity within your team. A diverse team brings a variety of perspectives and ideas, contributing to innovation and creativity.

20. **Continuous Learning Culture:**
- Cultivate a culture of continuous learning. Encourage your team to stay updated on industry trends and acquire new skills that benefit both individuals and the company.

In "Venture Ignition," the chapter on hiring and managing teams provides detailed insights and practical tips to help startups build and nurture high-performing teams. A well-managed team is a valuable asset for the growth and success of your startup.

9.1 Building a Strong Organizational Culture

Building a strong organizational culture is crucial for fostering a positive and productive work environment within a startup. Here's a guide to help you cultivate a robust organizational culture:

Define Core Values:

1. **Identify Core Values:**

- Clearly define the core values that represent the principles and beliefs of your startup. These values serve as the foundation for your organizational culture.

2. **Communicate Values Clearly:**
- Communicate your core values consistently and prominently. Ensure that every team member understands and embraces these values as guiding principles.

Leadership and Role Modeling:

3. **Leadership Commitment:**
- Demonstrate commitment to the organizational culture from the top down. Leadership sets the tone for the entire team, influencing behaviors and attitudes.

4. **Lead by Example:**
- Leaders should exemplify the values they promote. Consistent demonstration of desired behaviors encourages employees to follow suit.

Inclusive Environment:

5. **Embrace Diversity and Inclusion:**
- Foster an inclusive environment that values diversity. Embrace different perspectives, backgrounds, and experiences within your team.

6. **Open Communication:**
- Encourage open and transparent communication. Create avenues for team members to express their opinions, ideas, and concerns without fear of reprisal.

Employee Engagement:

7. **Recognition and Appreciation:**
- Recognize and appreciate the efforts of your team members. Regularly acknowledge achievements and milestones to boost morale.

8. **Professional Development:**
- Support the professional development of your employees. Provide opportunities for skill enhancement and career growth.

Team Collaboration:

9. **Encourage Collaboration:**
- Promote a collaborative working environment. Encourage teamwork, cross-functional collaboration, and knowledge sharing.

10. **Team-Building Activities:**

- Organize team-building activities that strengthen relationships and foster a sense of camaraderie. These activities can be both work-related and social.

Flexibility and Work-Life Balance:

11. **Flexible Work Arrangements:**
- Offer flexible work arrangements when possible. Supporting work-life balance demonstrates a commitment to the well-being of your team.

12. **Wellness Initiatives:**
- Implement wellness initiatives that support the physical and mental health of your employees. This can include health benefits, mindfulness programs, or fitness activities.

Continuous Learning:

13. **Learning Culture:**
- Cultivate a culture of continuous learning. Encourage curiosity and provide resources for ongoing education and development.

14. **Adaptability:**
- Embrace adaptability as a cultural trait. Encourage your team to be open to change and innovation, fostering a dynamic and responsive organization.

Values Integration:

15. **Integrate Values in Processes:**
- Integrate your core values into everyday processes. Ensure that they are reflected in decision-making, performance evaluations, and other organizational practices.

16. **Onboarding Integration:**
- Incorporate your organizational culture into the onboarding process for new hires. Help them understand and embody the values from the start.

Measure and Adjust:

17. **Employee Feedback:**
- Seek feedback from employees on the organizational culture. Regular surveys or open forums can provide insights for improvement.

18. **Continuous Evaluation:**
- Continuously evaluate the effectiveness of your organizational culture. Be willing to make adjustments based on feedback and evolving organizational needs.

In "Venture Ignition," the chapter on building organizational culture offers detailed insights and practical tips to help startups create a positive and resilient work culture. A strong organizational culture contributes to employee satisfaction, retention, and overall business success.

9.2 Leadership and Team Development

Leadership and team development are essential for fostering a high-performance culture within a startup. Here's a guide to help you cultivate effective leadership and build strong, cohesive teams:

Leadership Development:

1. **Identify Leadership Qualities:**
- Clearly define the leadership qualities and skills necessary for success within your startup. This could include communication, decision-making, adaptability, and strategic thinking.

2. **Leadership Training Programs:**
- Implement leadership training programs to develop and enhance these qualities. Offer workshops, coaching, or mentoring to support leadership growth.

3. **Lead by Example:**

- Leaders should exemplify the behavior and values expected from the team. Leading by example builds trust and credibility among team members.

4. **Continuous Learning:**
- Encourage leaders to engage in continuous learning. Staying updated on industry trends and leadership best practices contributes to effective decision-making.

5. **Feedback Mechanisms:**
- Establish feedback mechanisms for leadership. Regular evaluations and feedback from team members provide insights into leadership effectiveness.

Team Development:

6. **Define Team Goals:**
- Clearly define team goals aligned with the overall objectives of the startup. Teams should have a shared understanding of their purpose and desired outcomes.

7. **Collaborative Environment:**
- Foster a collaborative work environment where team members feel empowered to share ideas and contribute to the decision-making process.

8. **Team-Building Activities:**

- Organize team-building activities that enhance communication, trust, and cooperation. These activities can range from workshops to offsite retreats.

9. **Diversity and Inclusion:**
- Embrace diversity and inclusion within teams. Diverse teams bring a variety of perspectives and ideas, fostering creativity and innovation.

10. **Encourage Initiative:**
- Encourage team members to take initiative and lead projects or initiatives. Providing autonomy and recognizing individual contributions fosters a sense of ownership.

Communication:

11. **Open Communication Channels:**
- Establish open communication channels within the team. Regular team meetings, feedback sessions, and one-on-one discussions promote transparent communication.

12. **Active Listening:**
- Emphasize the importance of active listening. Leaders and team members should listen attentively to each other's ideas and concerns.

13. **Constructive Feedback:**
- Create a culture of constructive feedback. Encourage team members to provide feedback in a respectful manner and use feedback as a tool for improvement.

Conflict Resolution:

14. **Address Conflicts Promptly:**
- Address conflicts promptly and constructively. Establish protocols for conflict resolution to maintain a positive team dynamic.

15. **Mediation Skills:**
- Provide training in mediation skills for leaders. Developing the ability to mediate conflicts helps maintain a harmonious work environment.

Employee Recognition:

16. **Recognition Programs:**
- Implement employee recognition programs. Acknowledge and celebrate individual and team achievements to boost morale.

17. **Career Development Opportunities:**
- Offer career development opportunities within the team. Provide training, mentorship, and growth paths to retain and motivate team members.

Team Empowerment:

18. **Empowerment and Autonomy:**
- Empower teams with autonomy to make decisions within their areas of responsibility. This fosters a sense of ownership and accountability.

19. **Encourage Innovation:**
- Create an environment that encourages innovation. Team members should feel comfortable proposing and testing new ideas without fear of failure.

In "Venture Ignition," the chapter on leadership and team development provides detailed insights and practical tips to help startups nurture strong leadership and build cohesive, high-performing teams. Effective leadership and team dynamics are crucial for achieving long-term success and growth.

Chapter Ten
Scaling Your Business

Scaling a business involves strategic growth and expansion to meet increasing demand while maintaining efficiency and profitability. Here's a guide to help you navigate the process of scaling your startup:

Market Analysis:

1. **Identify Growth Opportunities:**
- Conduct a thorough analysis to identify new markets, customer segments, or product/service extensions that present growth opportunities.

2. **Assess Market Demand:**
- Evaluate the demand for your products or services in the target markets. Consider factors such as customer needs, competition, and market trends.

Operational Efficiency:

3. **Streamline Operations:**
- Optimize internal processes to enhance efficiency. This may involve automation, improved workflows, and the implementation of scalable technologies.

4. **Supply Chain Optimization:**

- Evaluate and optimize your supply chain to ensure it can handle increased production or service delivery. Strengthen relationships with suppliers and consider diversification.

Financial Planning:

5. **Financial Forecasting:**
- Develop comprehensive financial forecasts to anticipate capital requirements, revenue projections, and potential challenges associated with scaling.

6. **Secure Funding:**
- Identify funding sources to support your scaling efforts. This could include seeking investment, applying for loans, or exploring other financing options.

Team Expansion:

7. **Assess Workforce Needs:**
- Evaluate your current workforce and identify the skills and roles required for scaling. Consider hiring new talent or upskilling existing team members.

8. **Leadership Development:**
- Invest in leadership development to ensure your management team is equipped to lead the organization through growth and change.

Technology Adoption:

9. **Scalable Technology Solutions:**
- Implement scalable technology solutions that can support increased demand. This may include upgrading your IT infrastructure, adopting cloud services, or leveraging automation.

10. **Data Analytics:**
- Utilize data analytics to gather insights into customer behavior, market trends, and operational efficiency. Informed decision-making is crucial for successful scaling.

Customer Acquisition:

11. **Marketing and Sales Strategies:**
- Develop robust marketing and sales strategies to acquire new customers. This could involve expanding your online presence, entering new distribution channels, or launching targeted campaigns.

12. **Customer Retention:**
- Prioritize customer retention strategies to ensure the loyalty of existing customers. Happy customers can become advocates and contribute to organic growth.

Risk Management:

13. **Identify and Mitigate Risks:**
- Identify potential risks associated with scaling, such as supply chain disruptions, increased competition, or regulatory challenges. Develop risk mitigation plans to address these concerns.

14. **Scenario Planning:**
- Conduct scenario planning to anticipate different outcomes and responses to potential challenges. This proactive approach allows for better decision-making under various circumstances.

Measurement and Evaluation:

15. **Key Performance Indicators (KPIs):**
- Define and monitor key performance indicators (KPIs) that align with your scaling goals. Regularly assess these metrics to gauge the success of your expansion efforts.

16. **Continuous Improvement:**
- Foster a culture of continuous improvement. Regularly evaluate and adjust your strategies based on performance data, customer feedback, and market dynamics.

Legal and Compliance Considerations:

17. **Compliance Assessment:**
- Ensure compliance with relevant regulations and legal requirements in new markets. Conduct a thorough assessment to address any legal considerations associated with scaling.

18. **Intellectual Property Protection:**
- Assess and protect your intellectual property as you expand into new markets. This includes trademarks, patents, and copyrights.

In "Venture Ignition," the chapter on scaling your business provides detailed insights and practical tips to help startups navigate the complexities of expansion. A strategic and well-planned approach to scaling is crucial for sustained success in a competitive business landscape.

10.1 Expansion Strategies

Expansion strategies are crucial for startups looking to grow their reach and impact. Here's a guide to various expansion strategies that you can consider:

Market Expansion:

1. **Geographical Expansion:**
- Enter new geographical markets to tap into different customer bases. Conduct thorough market research to understand local preferences and adapt your products or services accordingly.

2. **Demographic Expansion:**
- Explore new customer demographics. Tailor your marketing and product strategies to appeal to different age groups, genders, or income levels.

Product or Service Expansion:

3. **Product Line Extension:**
- Introduce new products or expand your existing product line. This can cater to evolving customer needs and preferences.

4. **Service Diversification:**
- Diversify your service offerings to provide a broader range of solutions. This can enhance customer retention and attract a wider audience.

Channel Expansion:

5. **Online Presence Expansion:**

- Strengthen your online presence by expanding into new digital channels. This includes e-commerce platforms, social media, and other online marketplaces.

6. **Retail or Distribution Expansion:**
- Explore new retail partnerships or distribution channels. Collaborate with additional retailers or distributors to increase your product's availability.

Partnership and Collaboration:

7. **Strategic Partnerships:**
- Form strategic partnerships with other businesses. This could involve collaborations for joint ventures, co-marketing campaigns, or shared resources.

8. **Franchising:**
- Consider franchising your business model. Franchising allows others to replicate your successful model in different locations, often with lower risk for both parties.

Mergers and Acquisitions:

9. **Mergers:**
- Explore merger opportunities with other companies in your industry. Merging with a complementary

business can lead to synergies and increased market share.

10. **Acquisitions:**
- Acquire other businesses to expand your capabilities or enter new markets. This strategy can be effective for rapidly gaining a foothold in a specific industry or geography.

Licensing and Intellectual Property:

11. **Licensing Agreements:**
- Enter licensing agreements to allow other businesses to use your intellectual property, such as trademarks or patented technologies. This can generate revenue without the need for direct involvement.

International Expansion:

12. **Global Market Entry:**
- Consider expanding your operations internationally. This involves adapting your business model to fit the cultural, legal, and economic nuances of different countries.

Customer Retention and Upselling:

13. **Customer Loyalty Programs:**

- Implement customer loyalty programs to retain existing customers. Rewarding loyal customers can encourage repeat business and positive word-of-mouth.

14. **Upselling and Cross-selling:**
- Upsell additional products or services to existing customers. Cross-selling involves offering complementary products or services to enhance the customer's experience.

Innovation and Technology:

15. **Technology Integration:**
- Embrace new technologies to enhance your products or services. This could involve incorporating AI, IoT, or other cutting-edge technologies into your offerings.

16. **Innovation Centers:**
- Establish innovation centers within your organization to foster creativity and the development of new ideas. This can lead to breakthrough products or services.

Sustainability and Social Impact:

17. **Sustainable Practices:**

- Integrate sustainable practices into your business model. This can attract environmentally conscious consumers and contribute to a positive brand image.

18. **Social Impact Initiatives:**
- Engage in social impact initiatives or corporate social responsibility (CSR) programs. Aligning your business with a cause can resonate with socially conscious consumers.

In "Venture Ignition," the chapter on expansion strategies provides detailed insights and practical tips to help startups choose and implement the right strategies for sustainable growth. Each strategy should be carefully evaluated based on your business model, industry, and overall goals.

10.2 Adapting to Market Changes

Adapting to market changes is essential for the long-term success and sustainability of any startup. Here's a guide to help you navigate and respond effectively to shifts in the market:

Continuous Monitoring:

1. **Stay Informed:**

- Keep a pulse on industry news, trends, and market dynamics. Regularly monitor changes in consumer behavior, competitor activities, and external factors that may impact your business.

2. **Key Performance Indicators (KPIs):**
- Define and track key performance indicators (KPIs) relevant to your business. These metrics provide insights into your performance and can signal when adjustments are needed.

Flexibility and Agility:

3. **Cultivate Flexibility:**
- Foster a culture of flexibility within your organization. Encourage adaptability among your team members to respond quickly to changing circumstances.

4. **Agile Methodology:**
- Consider adopting agile methodologies in your project management processes. Agile practices enable quick adjustments and iterative improvements.

Customer Feedback and Engagement:

5. **Customer Feedback:**
- Actively seek and analyze customer feedback. Understand their needs, preferences, and any challenges

they may be facing. This insight is invaluable for making informed adjustments.

6. **Engage with Customers:**
- Regularly engage with your customer base through surveys, social media, and direct communication. Building strong relationships with customers can help you anticipate their evolving needs.

Strategic Planning:

7. **Scenario Planning:**
- Conduct scenario planning to anticipate different market scenarios. Develop strategies for potential challenges and opportunities that may arise in various situations.

8. **Regular Strategy Reviews:**
- Periodically review and reassess your business strategy. Ensure that it remains aligned with your long-term goals and is adaptable to changing market conditions.

Technology and Innovation:

9. **Embrace Technology:**
- Embrace technological advancements that can enhance your operations and offerings. Technology can

provide efficiency gains and open new avenues for growth.

10. **Invest in Innovation:**
- Allocate resources for innovation and research and development. Staying ahead of technological trends can position your startup as an industry leader.

Competitive Analysis:

11. **Competitor Monitoring:**
- Monitor your competitors closely. Analyze their strategies, product offerings, and market positioning. This information can inform your own strategic decisions.

12. **Competitive Advantage:**
- Identify and leverage your unique competitive advantage. Understanding what sets your startup apart allows you to capitalize on strengths and address weaknesses.

Financial Preparedness:

13. **Financial Resilience:**
- Maintain financial resilience by having contingency plans and a robust emergency fund. Financial stability

provides the flexibility to navigate unexpected challenges.

14. **Cost Management:**
- Regularly review and manage your costs. Identify areas where cost savings can be achieved without compromising the quality of your products or services.

Regulatory and Compliance:

15. **Stay Compliant:**
- Stay informed about changes in regulations and compliance requirements. Ensure that your startup adheres to legal standards to avoid potential setbacks.

16. **Adapt to Regulatory Changes:**
- Develop strategies to adapt to regulatory changes. Proactively address compliance issues to avoid disruptions to your operations.

Team Communication:

17. **Transparent Communication:**
- Maintain transparent communication within your team. Share information about market changes, challenges, and strategic shifts to keep everyone aligned.

18. **Team Collaboration:**

- Foster collaboration among team members. A collaborative environment encourages the sharing of ideas and solutions to navigate market changes effectively.

In "Venture Ignition," the chapter on adapting to market changes provides detailed insights and practical tips to help startups build resilience and agility. Adapting to market changes is a continuous process that requires a proactive and strategic approach.

Chapter Eleven
Overcoming Challenges and Learning from Failure

Overcoming challenges and learning from failure is an integral part of the entrepreneurial journey. Here's a guide to help you navigate challenges and turn failures into valuable learning experiences:

Resilience and Mindset:

1. **Cultivate Resilience:**
- Cultivate a resilient mindset to bounce back from setbacks. Understand that challenges are inevitable, but your ability to overcome them is crucial for long-term success.

2. **Positive Framing:**
- Frame challenges as opportunities for growth. Adopting a positive perspective can help you approach difficulties with a solution-oriented mindset.

Analyzing and Understanding Challenges:

3. **Root Cause Analysis:**
- Conduct a thorough analysis to identify the root causes of challenges. Understanding the underlying issues is essential for developing effective solutions.

4. **SWOT Analysis:**
- Perform a SWOT analysis (Strengths, Weaknesses, Opportunities, Threats) to assess your startup's internal and external factors. This analysis can inform your strategic decision-making.

Learning from Failure:

5. **Fail Fast, Learn Faster:**
- Embrace the concept of "fail fast, learn faster." Rapid iteration and learning from failures allow you to adapt quickly and make improvements.

6. **Post-Mortem Analysis:**
- After a setback, conduct a post-mortem analysis. Evaluate what went wrong, what worked well, and what lessons can be applied to future endeavors.

Adaptability and Flexibility:

7. **Embrace Adaptability:**
- Embrace adaptability as a core value. The ability to pivot and adjust your strategies based on new information or changing circumstances is crucial.

8. **Iterative Approach:**
- Adopt an iterative approach to your business model. Continuously test and refine your ideas based on feedback and market responses.

Seek Guidance and Mentorship:

9. **Mentorship:**

- Seek guidance from mentors who have experienced similar challenges. Their insights and advice can provide valuable perspectives and help you navigate difficult situations.

10. **Peer Networks:**
- Connect with other entrepreneurs and build a supportive peer network. Sharing experiences and learning from others' journeys can be enlightening and encouraging.

Strategic Decision-Making:

11. **Data-Informed Decisions:**
- Base your decisions on data and insights rather than emotions. Data-informed decision-making reduces the likelihood of repeating mistakes.

12. **Scenario Planning:**
- Engage in scenario planning to anticipate potential challenges. Developing contingency plans prepares you for unexpected events and minimizes the impact of setbacks.

Team Empowerment:

13. **Empower Your Team:**

- Empower your team to contribute ideas and
solutions. A collaborative approach ensures that
everyone is invested in overcoming challenges.

14. **Clear Communication:**
- Communicate openly with your team about
challenges. Transparent communication fosters trust and
enables collective problem-solving.

Continuous Learning:

15. **Learning Culture:**
- Foster a culture of continuous learning within your
startup. Encourage curiosity, experimentation, and a
willingness to learn from both successes and failures.

16. **Post-Success Analysis:**
- Even after successes, conduct analyses to understand
what contributed to success and what could be improved.
Continuous improvement is key to sustained growth.

Personal Reflection:

17. **Self-Reflection:**
- Engage in regular self-reflection. Assess your own
strengths and weaknesses, and be open to personal
development and growth.

18. **Embrace Feedback:**
- Embrace constructive feedback from peers, mentors, and customers. Feedback is a valuable tool for improvement and innovation.

In "Venture Ignition," the chapter on overcoming challenges and learning from failure provides detailed insights and practical tips to help startups build resilience and turn setbacks into stepping stones for success. Remember, challenges are not roadblocks but opportunities for growth and improvement.

11.1 Common Startup Pitfalls

Navigating the startup landscape comes with its challenges, and avoiding common pitfalls is crucial for success. Here's a guide to help you identify and steer clear of common startup pitfalls:

Lack of Market Research:

1. **Insufficient Market Understanding:**
- Pitfall: Launching a product or service without a clear understanding of the target market's needs, preferences, and pain points.
- Solution: Conduct thorough market research to validate your idea, identify your target audience, and assess market demand.

Weak Business Planning:

2. **Incomplete Business Plan:**
- Pitfall: Failing to develop a comprehensive business plan that outlines your value proposition, target market, revenue model, and growth strategy.
- Solution: Create a detailed business plan that serves as a roadmap for your startup, addressing key aspects of your business.

Inadequate Financial Management:

3. **Poor Financial Planning:**
- Pitfall: Neglecting financial planning, leading to cash flow issues, overspending, and financial instability.
- Solution: Develop realistic financial projections, monitor expenses, and establish a financial contingency plan to ensure fiscal responsibility.

Overlooking Legal Considerations:

4. **Neglecting Legal Compliance:**
- Pitfall: Ignoring legal requirements, such as business registrations, licenses, and compliance with industry regulations.

- Solution: Consult with legal professionals to ensure your startup complies with all relevant laws and regulations.

Team Challenges:

5. **Ineffective Team Building:**
- Pitfall: Building a team without considering skills, cultural fit, and communication dynamics, leading to internal conflicts and inefficiencies.
- Solution: Invest time in hiring the right talent, fostering a positive team culture, and promoting effective communication.

Ignoring Customer Feedback:

6. **Disregarding Customer Input:**
- Pitfall: Failing to actively seek and incorporate customer feedback, resulting in products or services that don't align with market needs.
- Solution: Establish feedback loops, engage with customers regularly, and use insights to refine your offerings.

Scaling Too Quickly:

7. **Premature Scaling:**

- Pitfall: Scaling operations, team, or resources too quickly without a solid foundation, leading to financial strain and operational challenges.
- Solution: Prioritize sustainable growth, carefully assess scalability, and ensure your startup is ready for expansion.

Lack of Marketing Strategy:

8. **Ineffective Marketing:**
- Pitfall: Not having a clear and effective marketing strategy, which can hinder customer acquisition and brand visibility.
- Solution: Develop a targeted marketing plan, leverage digital channels, and align your marketing efforts with your overall business goals.

Resistance to Adaptation:

9. **Failure to Pivot:**
- Pitfall: Being resistant to change or not recognizing the need to pivot when market conditions or customer preferences evolve.
- Solution: Stay agile, monitor market trends, and be willing to adjust your business model based on feedback and changing circumstances.

Insufficient Focus on Value Proposition:

10. **Unclear Value Proposition:**
- Pitfall: Failing to clearly communicate the unique value your startup offers, making it challenging to stand out in the market.
- Solution: Define and articulate your value proposition, emphasizing what sets your product or service apart from competitors.

Lack of Networking and Partnerships:

11. **Isolation from the Ecosystem:**
- Pitfall: Operating in isolation without building a network or forming strategic partnerships that can enhance growth opportunities.
- Solution: Actively engage with industry networks, attend events, and explore collaboration opportunities to broaden your reach.

Inadequate Risk Management:

12. **Ignoring Risks:**
- Pitfall: Not proactively identifying and managing potential risks, leaving your startup vulnerable to unforeseen challenges.
- Solution: Conduct risk assessments regularly, develop risk mitigation plans, and be prepared to adapt to unexpected circumstances.

In "Venture Ignition," the chapter on common startup pitfalls provides detailed insights and practical advice to help startups avoid these challenges and navigate the path to success more effectively. Being aware of these pitfalls and proactively addressing them can significantly contribute to the resilience and sustainability of your startup.

11.2 Resilience and Growth Mindset

Resilience and a growth mindset are key attributes that can contribute significantly to the success of an entrepreneur and their startup. Let's explore each of these qualities:

Resilience:

1. **Definition:**
- Resilience is the ability to bounce back from setbacks, adapt to change, and persevere in the face of challenges. It involves maintaining a positive mindset and emotional well-being during difficult times.

2. **Importance for Entrepreneurs:**
- In the unpredictable world of startups, challenges are inevitable. Resilient entrepreneurs can navigate setbacks

more effectively, learning from experiences and using adversity as a catalyst for growth.

3. **Characteristics of Resilient Entrepreneurs:**
- **Optimism:** Resilient entrepreneurs maintain an optimistic outlook, focusing on solutions rather than dwelling on problems.
- **Adaptability:** They embrace change and adapt their strategies when faced with unexpected circumstances.
- **Perseverance:** Resilient individuals persevere through difficulties, staying committed to their goals despite obstacles.

4. **Cultivating Resilience:**
- **Self-Care:** Prioritize self-care to maintain physical and mental well-being.
- **Learning from Setbacks:** View failures as opportunities for learning and growth.
- **Building a Support System:** Surround yourself with a supportive network of mentors, advisors, and peers.

Growth Mindset:

1. **Definition:**
- A growth mindset is the belief that one's abilities and intelligence can be developed through dedication, hard

work, and learning. Individuals with a growth mindset see challenges as opportunities to learn and improve.

2. **Importance for Entrepreneurs:**
- Entrepreneurs with a growth mindset are more likely to embrace challenges, persist in the face of setbacks, and continuously seek opportunities for learning and improvement.

3. **Characteristics of Entrepreneurs with a Growth Mindset:**
- **Openness to Learning:** They are eager to learn from experiences, feedback, and new information.
- **Embracing Challenges:** Instead of avoiding challenges, they see them as opportunities for personal and professional development.
- **Effort as a Path to Mastery:** They understand that effort and dedication lead to mastery and success.

4. **Cultivating a Growth Mindset:**
- **Embrace Challenges:** Approach challenges with a positive attitude, seeing them as chances to learn and grow.
- **Learn from Criticism:** View constructive criticism as valuable feedback for improvement.

Chapter Twelve
Conclusion

In conclusion, embarking on the entrepreneurial journey requires a combination of strategic planning, resilience, a growth mindset, and the ability to adapt to changing circumstances. "Venture Ignition" serves as a comprehensive guide, offering insights and practical advice to help startups navigate the challenges and opportunities that come their way.

From the importance of market research and effective business planning to the need for resilience and a growth mindset, each chapter provides valuable guidance for entrepreneurs seeking success in the competitive startup landscape. By understanding common pitfalls, learning from failure, and embracing continuous improvement, startup founders can build a strong foundation for sustainable growth.

As you embark on your venture, remember the significance of cultivating a positive and adaptive organizational culture, fostering strong leadership, and building cohesive teams. Whether you are developing expansion strategies, overcoming challenges, or adapting to market changes, the principles outlined in "Venture Ignition" are designed to support you in building a resilient and successful startup.

In the dynamic and ever-evolving world of entrepreneurship, the ability to learn, adapt, and persevere is paramount. May your entrepreneurial journey be marked by innovation, tenacity, and the fulfillment of your vision. Best of luck on your venture, and may it ignite a path to lasting success.

12.1 Celebrating Milestones

Celebrating milestones is a crucial aspect of recognizing and appreciating the progress your startup has made. Here's a guide to help you commemorate achievements and foster a positive and motivated team culture:

1. **Define Milestones:**
- Clearly define and set measurable milestones for your startup. These could include product launches, customer acquisition goals, revenue targets, or other significant achievements.

2. **Acknowledge Small Wins:**
- Celebrate not only major milestones but also small victories along the way. Recognizing incremental successes boosts morale and encourages a positive mindset.

3. **Team Recognition:**

- Acknowledge the collective effort of your team. Celebrate milestones as team achievements, highlighting the collaborative spirit that contributes to your startup's success.

4. **Personalized Recognition:**
- Provide personalized recognition to team members who played a pivotal role in reaching specific milestones. This could include a simple thank-you note, a public acknowledgment, or a small token of appreciation.

5. **Celebration Events:**
- Organize celebration events to mark significant milestones. This could be a team outing, a virtual celebration, or a themed event that aligns with the achievement.

6. **Share Success Stories:**
- Share success stories internally and externally. Whether through newsletters, social media, or internal communications, highlight the journey and the milestones achieved.

7. **Reflect and Learn:**
- Take the time to reflect on the journey leading to the milestone. Discuss what worked well, what challenges

were overcome, and what lessons can be learned for future endeavors.

8. **Recognition Programs:**
- Establish recognition programs within your startup. Consider monthly or quarterly awards for outstanding contributions, innovation, or dedication to achieving milestones.

9. **Gratitude and Appreciation:**
- Express gratitude and appreciation for the hard work and dedication of your team. A simple "thank you" can go a long way in fostering a positive and motivated work environment.

10. **Showcase Milestones Visually:**
- Create visual representations of milestones, such as charts, graphs, or a timeline. Display these visuals in common areas or during team meetings to keep everyone informed and motivated.

11. **Future Goals:**
- Connect milestone celebrations with future goals. Use the momentum from achieving one milestone to set new, ambitious targets that inspire continued dedication and innovation.

12. **Involve the Entire Team:**

- Involve the entire team in the celebration planning process. This not only ensures that celebrations resonate with the team but also fosters a sense of ownership and camaraderie.

13. **Feedback and Suggestions:**
- Solicit feedback and suggestions from team members on how they would like to celebrate milestones. Incorporating their ideas enhances engagement and enthusiasm.

14. **Continuous Recognition:**
- Implement a culture of continuous recognition. Regularly acknowledge individual and team efforts, creating a positive atmosphere that extends beyond specific milestones.

15. **Client and Customer Appreciation:**
- Extend celebrations to include client and customer appreciation. Recognize their role in your success and express gratitude for their ongoing support.

Celebrating milestones not only boosts morale and motivation but also reinforces a positive company culture. By recognizing and appreciating the efforts of your team, you create an environment that encourages continuous dedication and achievement. In "Venture Ignition," the chapter on celebrating milestones provides detailed insights and practical tips to help startups create meaningful and impactful celebrations.

12.2 Looking Ahead: The Continuous Evolution of Your Business

Looking ahead to the continuous evolution of your business is a critical aspect of long-term success. Here's a guide to help you navigate the ongoing development and growth of your startup:

1. **Strategic Planning:**
- Regularly revisit and update your business strategy. Consider changes in market conditions, customer preferences, and industry trends to ensure your strategy remains relevant.

2. **Market Research:**
- Stay attuned to market changes through continuous market research. Understanding shifts in the industry landscape allows you to proactively adapt your products or services.

3. **Customer Feedback Loop:**
- Establish a continuous feedback loop with your customers. Actively seek input on your offerings, customer experience, and areas for improvement.

4. **Innovation and R&D:**
- Invest in innovation and research and development
(R&D). Embrace new technologies, explore creative
solutions, and strive to stay ahead of industry
advancements.

5. **Agile Management Practices:**
- Adopt agile management practices. This involves
being flexible, responsive to change, and capable of
making quick and effective decisions.

6. **Talent Development:**
- Focus on the continuous development of your team.
Offer training programs, mentorship opportunities, and a
supportive environment that encourages skill
enhancement.

7. **Diversification:**
- Explore diversification opportunities. This could
involve expanding your product line, entering new
markets, or diversifying revenue streams to mitigate
risks.

8. **Technology Integration:**
- Embrace technological advancements. Incorporate
emerging technologies that can enhance your operations,
improve efficiency, and provide a competitive edge.

9. **Strategic Partnerships:**
- Form strategic partnerships. Collaborate with other businesses to leverage complementary strengths and access new markets or resources.

10. **Sustainability Practices:**
- Integrate sustainability practices into your business model. Addressing environmental and social concerns can enhance your brand reputation and resonate with socially conscious consumers.

11. **Data-Driven Decision-Making:**
- Embrace data-driven decision-making. Utilize analytics to gather insights into customer behavior, operational efficiency, and market trends.

12. **Crisis Preparedness:**
- Develop crisis preparedness plans. Anticipate potential challenges and have contingency plans in place to navigate unforeseen circumstances effectively.

13. **International Expansion:**
- Consider international expansion. Assess opportunities and challenges in global markets, and tailor your strategies to fit the cultural and economic nuances of different regions.

14. **Continuous Brand Building:**

- Continuously build and evolve your brand. Ensure that your brand messaging aligns with your values and resonates with your target audience.

15. **Evaluating Competition:**
- Regularly evaluate your competition. Stay informed about their strategies, products, and market positioning to identify areas for differentiation and improvement.

16. **Regulatory Compliance:**
- Stay updated on regulatory changes. Regularly assess and ensure compliance with relevant laws and regulations that may impact your business.

17. **Scenario Planning:**
- Engage in scenario planning. Anticipate future scenarios, assess potential risks, and develop strategies to navigate different outcomes.

18. **Customer-Centric Approach:**
- Maintain a customer-centric approach. Understand evolving customer needs and preferences, and adjust your offerings and services accordingly.

19. **Continuous Improvement Culture:**
- Foster a culture of continuous improvement. Encourage your team to identify areas for enhancement and contribute to the ongoing evolution of the business.

Looking ahead involves a proactive and strategic approach to ensure your startup remains adaptable and resilient in a dynamic business environment. In "Venture Ignition," the chapter on the continuous evolution of your business provides detailed insights and practical tips to help startups navigate the challenges of ongoing development and growth. Remember, the ability to evolve is key to sustaining success in the ever-changing landscape of entrepreneurship.